A LENS TO SEE BEHIND THE SKY

A Lens to See Behind the Sky
5x8 First Edition
978-0-9984381-6-0
Published by Secret Midnight Press

www.secretmidnightpress.com
www.ashleydun.com

A LENS TO SEE BEHIND THE SKY

ashley dun

PREFACE.

If you've ever felt the weight of existence burying you deep underground, you're in the right place. If you've ever sat alone all night wondering why you're still alive, wondering what it all means, wondering if any of this is real, you're in the right place. If you've ever suffered only because others are suffering (the empath), we're in this together. You're not alone. Throughout this book of poetry, words will form metaphors and similes and images of longing for death. This is how I fight those thoughts. This book is my battle ground. Not every poem will end on a hopeful note, but it means I conquered the darkness, at least for the moment. It is easy to become overwhelmed by the weight of life, but you must never let it take you. Find your way to fight it. Use words, a paintbrush, an instrument, anything to remember you have control over creating your story.

Please know that although the endings aren't always hopeful, they've pulled at the rope around my neck to loosen the grip and I feel a sense of freedom. Please know that this can happen for you too. Please know that you're not alone in this fight. I'm right here with you.

I will leave you with musings I wrote down during the process of creating this book:

Sometimes I sit and daydream about what it would be like to live a quiet life. To have a quiet mind, a heart that sleeps soundly at night. I am truly envious of those who are able to walk through life without soaking up the sorrow of it all. I absorb all around me. It's beauty and it's suffering and it's hard to find balance.

Depression isn't just feeling 'sad'. It's not always related to circumstances. It's not an equation to solve. Someone once asked me if I knew what the root of my depression is. I told them I wish there was one. Because if there were roots, I could pull them out of the ground and be free. Instead it's a component of the soil, a natural element that I'm not sure I'll ever have the tools to remove.

Recognizing this is not a white flag of defeat. No, I'm shaking hands with it and agreeing to work with it. I'm agreeing to row against the rushing current because there are calm waters ahead.

Some days I'm fighting. Some days I'm soaking in the sun. Others I let the rain come down on me and I weep with the sky. It's a cycle just like everything is a cycle. We rotate together.

What calms me is that I'm not in this alone. what calms me is that there are people who understand. what I'll never know is why some people don't try to understand. I'm jealous of the people who don't have to.

In the meantime I look for speckled sunlight, rays floating through leafy branches, the rustling of life when the wind comes. I know that the earth suffers with me. We're aware of the weight and fragility of existence.

As a feather on a bird's wing, we're here for a brief moment but we are involved in the movement. Sometimes I sit and daydream about what it would be like to live a quiet life. I'll find my peace in soaring wings.

My deepest thanks to family & friends for your endless support.
To my husband, my lifeline, Andrew Lee
To my family Laura, Bill, Abigail, Jordan & Joshua Dun
To soul friends AJD, DAP, EAD, ECK, ERK, EAW, JCB, RRS, & RJB

Layout by Jason Turner
Pages 127-137, Artwork by Emma Ruff
Black & white photos taken of & by Ashley's Great-Grandfather William S. Dun
Typewriter words hand-typed by Ashley Dun

CONTENTS.

PART 1 / SMOKE SIGNALS (BURN THIS)

PART 2 / WIND WHISPERING SECRETS
FEW HAVE EARS TO HEAR

PART 3 / THE MOODS OF DEEPEST ROOTS

PART 4 / CURIOSITIES CALLED OUT
FROM LEAGUES UNDER THE SEA

A LENS TO SEE BEHIND THE SKY

do you
see your galaxies?
you walk through
the fire before you
blazing it binds
instead of burns
do you
see your galaxies?
the earth welcomes
your warm feet
feels your fingers when
you dig in and makes
you one from which
you came
do you
see your galaxies?
each gust of wind
breathes a grateful
purpose into
your being
do you
see your galaxies?
like sea
dust you
shimmer in
the light and you're
reminded of
every
reason
you choose
to be alive.
do you?

PART I

SMOKE SIGNALS
(BURN THIS)

SMOKE SIGNALS

what you didn't know
is that you handed me
the match
that day you left me with
your words like oil
dripping down
my skin and pooling
at my feet until I'm
drowning in the dark
screaming your name and
what you didn't know
is that your breath
was the heat that
called the spark a flame
until I'm nothing but
a blaze
brief and building
a tower of haze climbing
toward the stars and
what you didn't know
is that now
my dark and greying
glow will
be the one to
guide them
home

1

it's just that
the way your name tastes
in my mouth is like
cotton candy on a hot summer day
melting sugar on my tongue and
it's just that
the rough edges around your fingers
remind me of sand on my skin
foamy tide washing over me and
it's just that
the sun can't stay and
the green leaves are fleeting
and you can't promise me you won't
leave like the summer
and come back resurrected and
our love is a sunset,
a death so beautiful I forget
my sorrow and
it's just that
nothing
lovely
lasts

2

when you think of me
do you remember the way I
held you when you were a shaking
leaf in a storm
do you remember when I forgave you
every
single
time
and how my love for you stretched
from my soul all the way
around the universe and
back to cradle your heart
do you remember the way I
looked at you in the dim light
damp from dancing in the rain
and the wrinkles by my eyes from
the way we were invincible until
we weren't or until
you chose them over me
do you remember how I
moved on but never let you know
that I remember
every breath and beating and
I hate you for living in the corners of
my mind and I'll never forgive you
for never letting me go

3

I am drenched in
life and dehydrated from
living
and I can't find
ground to stand on when
I see every life I'm not living
and I am constantly crushed by the
monotony of the life I am
living and I can't even
breathe with this
toxic air of unhappiness
and fear and
each day is our last because
no one will ever know which
breath is our last
so I cry out for meaning
and I dig my fingernails
into the soil because
it's the only thing that's real and
I'm not ready to let go of this
reality because it's all I know and
I'm not ready to give in to
what I don't know so feet
don't fail me now
lets run until the horizon blurs
and the heat of the sun burns
and please
let me die by
the fire
of life

4

my
mind is
a minefield so
don't wander too far
or the ground will
burst like blood
vessels before
bruises chaos
created by lack
of light
limping through the
dark alleys of
me
lost and
lonely and I beg
you
to keep your distance
safe and sterile and soft
clean and calm you
don't need these burn marks so
march forward through
foot-worn paths far
far away from
me

5

I heard our song and then
your hands were
on mine
holding them above
my head and
your hot breath on my neck in
mid-summer
fireworks crawling across
the sky outside but
we didn't need anything else to
tell us we were alive as
the record spun like a web
around us and we
thought we
we're safe.
I heard our song and then
my hands were
in fists pounding on
your chest
screaming how
how could you leave me like
this like the summer sun
setting in late September like
the smoke from your
cigarettes left a
scent I can never get out

6

my mind is
melting out of my ears
candle wax dripping under a
flickering fire
and oh how I long for rain

7

I wish I could
crawl inside your chest
curled up behind your
ribs and tucked between
your lungs I would
swim in the
sea of you.
I wish I could
see through your skull
like a window
and hold your thoughts
in my palms like a
pearl sparkling in
the sunlight.
I wish I could
breathe beauty
through you until
it runs through your
veins like a river and
oh how you beautifully
you burn
while I die as the
match that lit you

8

I spill like
a waterfall
over you
breaking
underneath you
and taking
pieces of you
with me.
I fill like
a well during
a storm when
you breathe
hot fire on my
neck and
it hurts
the way you
land like broken glass
on my back.
I kill like
a starving hunter
in winter
until your
blood runs in
pools with
my own
until I'm still
like a gazelle in the
crosshairs of your
gun
frozen at the
finality of my
fate

9

there is a bird
bright and beautiful
that lives within me
some days he sings for me
soft and sweet
his melody flows out of me
like rays of light through clouds
some days he sleeps softly
his presence forgotten and I
rest with him
some days he will slowly
stretch his wings
signaling his suffering
I feel his sorrow filling me like
smoke and
some days his cage feels like
it's shrinking and
he lifts his wings
flapping them violently within me
his futile efforts shaking me to the core
and my heart aches for him because
he, like me,
will never be free

what is Your Secret?

quel est ton secret?

10

you are the first
sip of coffee
and the last
sip of tea
everything about you
envelops me

11

sometimes my brain
crawls into a dusty corner
clawing through the dark and
I think how odd it is that maybe
in the same bed
that I was born in
a person
died.
the same blue scrubs
hovering over his
hollow body in the
same spot that
my existence began and
we both stepped out
screaming.
sometimes my brain
wanders into waters too deep
struggling to breathe and
I think how my life is
as fleeting as a
moth's wing
drawn to the light
not realizing
it's fire and I'm
doused in
gasoline.

12

I am haunted
your spirit lingers
in between my bones
your voice echoing through
the dark cavities of me
crawling through my
crevices
you whisper all
of the words that
only we knew and
I am haunted
by the smoke after
fireworks on that hot
summer night
by your warm breath whispering
words that ring
painful and shrill in my ears and
long for you
to set me free

13

our love was like hot breath on cold glass
fingers tracing hearts
x's and o's
bodies knotted together in the
back seat of my silver car the
rain coming down on us like
a whisper but all we felt
was fire
eyes full of each other and
our veins were electric as we
swayed like a boat on the waves
as we forgot the beauty of the
dying leaves outside
and for a moment
you were all there was
and for a moment time stopped,
the rain went back into the sky and
the fog cleared
until your name written on the window
disappeared
smoke and vapors like a dream
but I cling onto the mist
hoping you'll miss me again and
I'll be here
waiting for your voice like spring
a sure thing that never
fails to
fail me in
the end

14

red wine lips and
paint stroke stumbles
wooden warrior
moving through time like
branches in the wind
feel the flowers curl in the cold
fingers frozen buried in pockets
and your soul shrinks
autumn leaves bleed for me
dying for my sins
to be resurrected again
after white death's cool whisper
so close to taking your soul
chilling to the bone
but you know
winter
won't
win

15

if only
the sky would
swallow me up
making me into
raindrops like
clouds bleeding make
new life
out of nothing
if only
the earth would
crawl up around me
letting me rest
in the dust that I
came from like
mountains always
melt into sand
if only
I could pull apart
putting pieces of myself
in places they fit like
puzzle pieces like
stars scatter
to make constellations
if only
my light would reflect
like sun
rays on stained
glass like mirrors
whisper lies
disguised as truth
telling you
if only

16

I see the universe when I
close my eyes
nothing but
grey when they're open
each foot in a different world
one weighed down by gravity
and the other floats like
sparkles in the sea
my head lives in the clouds
my feet among the roots of
ancient trees and
my body aches with each
day being pulled between
dreams and reality

17

your voice is like
honey
dripping down
my throat
but your words like
daggers make me
bleed
so stop
calling my name
in your sleep
because
each cut is curing my
disease of you
draining the illness
of needing you
despite the condition of my
cardiac muscle
every time you
tell me that you
love me because
lord knows
these letters are
lies and
lord knows
I need more
than vows from vowels so please
forgive me and
forget me
while we
sway to the dance of the
devil
while we

weep with each breath
whispering
goodbye

18

these years like
paint strokes sweep by in
patterns I hadn't imagined.
words like
'tranquilizers' are
triggers and the smell of
smoke takes me
to you.
my thoughts fill my head like
water and I'm
drowning in
your goodbye.

19

one year has passed
since you buried yourself in
my soul
made a home underneath my skin
and even though you're gone
you've left behind pieces of you
shrapnel from the war and
it hurts when I move a certain way
your remnants dig into my flesh
and a flash
a picture of you blinds me and
I'm broken down again
you left your pieces and
you took some of mine with
you and
I will never be the same

Dearest Binx,

When you hug me, you hold my head close to your chest.
There are ways in which you are perfectly wrong for me.
This is not one of them. You send me notes in the early
morning while I dream. before the sun rises. These words
form the string that wraps me around your finger. Despite
the broken lines that create our connection, the list of
dont's that apply to you, my thoughts drift often to you.
My heart should not be this magnetic.

I look into the mirror and see a shadow of a person; a
vague, dark silhouette, longing to be filled in and made
whole. When will this fog clear? My energy is waning like
the winter sun. I am at a crossroads, but the clouds are
low and dense. This grey, milky sky is making my vision
dim. disguising my options to make at this fork in the
road.

Is it obvious to you my fear of falling in love? Perhaps
I'm confused, blinded by this fog, by you. Can you hear
my heart breaking? Maybe last night you heard the sound
like standing on ice in early spring. Maybe you sensed
the changing seasons when we first met.

Is it too late for us? How many times canI say I'm sorry
before the scars start to fade? My broken heart is leaving
a trail of wounds in its wake, and I am in your debt.

Forever,
Bambi

20

maybe it wasn't for us
you know
this life
the one where sunrises and
sunsets are so beautiful it
hurts like the razor edge of a
snowflake and
maybe it wasn't for us
the strings of the violin that
vibrate in the softest way to melt
our hearts but
despite the songs you
sang me
the poems you wrote me
the hands on the clock moved in
such a way to call us
elsewhere
away from one another
though it hurts but
in the end
maybe it wasn't for us
the way our skin bonded like
hot metal to plastic
broken pieces of glass
into art
light glowing through it but
maybe it wasn't for us
this life
so I'll be the
one in red
waiting
in the next

21

when you look at me
I feel the freckles of your eyes
like shadows repelling the
sun from my skin
and when you say my name
I feel the letters wrap around me
like barbed wire and
when you hold her it's like
a hot shower on a cold day
singeing the feeling from my skin
fiery release
I burn at the stake so that you
can be free

22

god it hurts
I read these words
that I spewed out like
sewage and
god I'm sick
my soul looks like
the flowers you gave me
weeks ago and like
the words you wrote me
months ago that once meant
something and now
the shapes of the letters are
cold like coffins
flowerbeds in fall
and all I need is for you to
not need me and
all I want is for you to
want me

23

is this what living looks like?
like there's this gaping
wound in my chest
like salt water
washed over it and
breathing is more like
gasping and
this can't be what living looks like.
like the night never ends
and the stars have been
eaten alive by
the black sky and
I'll never know
why the sun never seems
to rise in the places my
eyes look upon through
broken glasses.
this won't be what living looks like.
I will sew up my shattered
spirit with twine and
I will
be my own light.
I will
be a spark to
ignite the sun and
defeat the
cold dark of night.

24

do you ever get tired of
communicating?
like it's pulling teeth and each
tooth is a precious gem to
you like
it's giving birth
but you didn't choose to
hurt like this to
be born in the first place and
recreating is just
shedding skin
till you're raw and new
but still
no one sees you
the way you
long to be seen.
do you ever get tired of
communicating?
because words will never
suffice for the
hurricane of
feelings for the
tornado of
bleeding you feel
inside of you constantly
swirling in your
milky way mind but
all they see are
raindrops on silky
sea water while the
rest of you spins on into eternity
because

communicating
can never
cure the sickness of
language the disease
of desire to
shed your skin to
be truly seen to
be truly heard.
do you ever get tired of
communicating?

25

my fragile frame can barely
stand the changing winds
chilling each bone like
icy fingertips on the tongue
and it hurts to breathe
but you wouldn't know that
by my white teeth
though the shape of my back
suggests the weight I am carrying
the cross I am bearing
both your sins and mine
and you've left me with them all
while the breeze whispers your name
and my dreams haunt me with
my eyes open and closed

26

my fingernails
are filled
with dirt from
trying to
climb out of
the grave you
gave me
that day you
took my breath
without
returning it

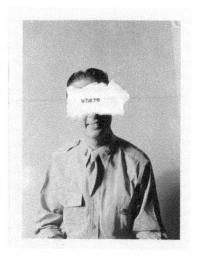

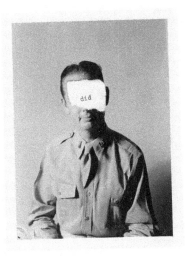

27

for a moment I thought
the sky was whispering
sweet secrets to soothe
my scarred soul
the outlines of the clouds like
mountains make me
feel renewed and
for a moment I thought
I would be okay like
the light blue loved me
more than I ever could until
I blinked my heavy
eyelids and the blue turned
black

28

strange
how two souls connect
can weave into each other
a tapestry of memory
songs and silhouettes
taste and touch
melt into one bleeding
ink sketch dripping with
salt water seared into
your thoughts until you breathe
your final breath
these two separate souls
heart beats stagger and split
flesh on flesh
scream sorrow as the cords
drop and fray
slow motion walk away
hollowness left where this
once intimate creature held
you close is now nothing but a
stranger.

29

your lips leave a taste like
metal on mine
that dull taste of
blood
and I can't stop
tonguing the wound
a pain so familiar
so intimate
and I'd rather feel
this ache than
nothing at all
but oh god you hold me like
a cocoon and I am
transformed
set free and
your embrace
tastes like the
sunrise after
a storm
but if you could only see
the power
you have over me
you would feel the ground
shaking beneath me and the
sky weighing down on me
like a stone
and oh god how I wish I felt
nothing at all

30

today
I painted the town red
and it splattered in lines
across my wrists
while I sacrifice myself
at the altar of
my culture
raging against the bright
fire of life
swallowing my soul
until all that remains
is smoke and
I break like
hot glass under cold water
when I reach out
further than my soul can stretch
so instead I dig in
fingers in the dirt so
my veins feed into the
roots and I am
healed from this
shattered system that
slices through the core
of me while I
bleed out the
red sickness of being until
I am finally
free

31

when you say my name
I see the letters trickling
off your lips like
blood
spilling out of you like
a sickness
and I'm so
sorry
for calling you
cursed like
anyone who has
looked at me with
hungry eyes
will never
leave satisfied

32

I live in a cage
of language and longing
flowers trying to bloom
in a dark dry corner
fire in a volcano that
will never erupt
and the stars laugh
never letting me feel them
they're bright but not blinding
beautiful but distant
and I understand them
watching the world from afar
words failing me
my heart betraying me
I'm banging against these walls
but my fists hurt from fighting it
there's no key that will unlock my misery
so I wait
for life to escape me
my spirit set free from feeling

33

the world has lost its color
greens and blues sucked from
the veins it is now
pale and lifeless
cold, unwelcoming
small cracks split my skin and
and joy seeps out
I have lost my color
bones like ice
sharp and jagged
I fear myself
what I will become
when I thaw

34

it hurts too much
the glow is dim and
the fire failing
I am thirsty for life
my eyes hunger and my
flesh longs for discovery
introspective inspiration
and an explosion of emotion
I won't settle for the cracks
in this land the filthy features
of my surroundings
surrendering to
the inevitable and I am
incapable of healing
without change and
god I need your fix and I'm
broken without your breath in
my lungs

35

how many
shades of blue
do you see when I speak
when I close my eyes
the tides sigh around me
the skies cry tears like
water on words
blurring ink
black dripping
down to my heels
blood before it leaves my
veins showing through
my weary flesh my
shades of blue
are calming to you
but you can't see how my
shades of blue
are slowly killing me

hollow

how low?

36

my thoughts swirl around me
wrapping me up with their
barbed wire and
I'm bleeding words
hot emotion oozing and
pooling at my feet and
no one can see it
only I am left here to
drown in the poison
I created for myself;
a subtle suicide
for the paralyzed poet.

37

it's like a snake has been
slithering up my spine
since birth
slowly wrapping its silky body
around mine, numbing
and tonguing my spirit like
a morning frost.
shiny black
burning cold to the
touch but
I've lost the feeling
in my fingers so
I know that I'm
numb and somehow the
chill is welcome
calling me into the quiet
blackness
binding me in its
coils whispering
it'll be over soon
it'll be over soon

38

I feel like I'm crawling
in an endless dark I'm on
black gravel and my
bleeding palms pull me
forward into the neon night.
the air is heavy,
there is nothing before me so I
could curl up in
the cracked earth or I
could skid my skin across
these crude rocks and I'm
not sure I will survive and I'm
not sure I want to

39

sometimes it hurts
to put these words on
the page like
an amputation
from my brain
pieces of my soul
        falling out like
  raindrops until I
no longer
exist

40

what happens to the words
'I love you'
once they've spilled out
of your mouth like
that time we rolled down
the soft green hill
laughing and our
bruises became
landmarks like
grass stains will
always remind me of
those hot summer days
with you and ever since
you said those words
it's like they floated off with
the smoke from your cigarette so
how can I hold onto them
turning them into soft clay in my
hands to mold with
warmth and make them
mean something again

41

I drink darkness like
ink
spills slowly through
my veins until
I bleed black and
its silky sorrow
weaving a web
fills each fiber
with weight like
iron and shapes
like shackles
surround each strand
of my DNA
pulling me six
feet underground but
I know I am
stronger than your
secret syringes
stealing life from
my veins until
my flesh turns to earth so
until then I will
fight
against the darkness like
a sunrise
shattering night and
even when it seems like the
black is burying me
I will rise
with the
spring roses
out of snow

42

you are the sun breaking
through drawn blinds strewn
across these walls dancing
through veiny leaves embracing
every inch of my being
and you call me whole
you ignite the moon keeping
me from utter darkness guiding
me through the night like
a ship in a storm pulling
me into your arms
and I call you home

43

never get comfortable with mental illness
it is not your friend
it is a force you must fight
I know the heat is like home
burning embers on your flesh and
you know you're alive but
you can't let it consume
all the crevices of you because
there is life where water runs
cool across your feet
rapid and royal it
breathes life into your bones
unlike this smoke that smothers you
like wool on a warm night.
never get comfortable with mental illness
or it'll steal your soul when
you least suspect it so
seek the light
brave like morning
bursting through darkness and
hold on for the new
if the sun can do it
so can you.

44

it's like I woke up one morning broken
my porcelain shattered and
I sewed up my skin like
silk but it never looked
the same.
it's like I woke up one morning boring
my bright dulled and my
petals wilted
like I'm a drawing that's been
erased
a shadow of me left
pieces swept away in the wind.
it's like I woke up one morning bleeding
it leaks out of me like lava
a burning blessing
and each day I'm deflating
oxygen sneaking out until
I'm nothing but for now
I will wake up each morning bolder
brought to life by the light
and like a wildflower in winter
I will always fight

hollow

how low?

45

what if I don't live to be
ninety
but oh god
what if I do?
do I want to see the world through weary eyes
death sleeping next to me
and life seeping out of the cracks?
I feel the weight of
each second
like a boulder burying me so
instead of having
ninety
years I hope to have
ninety
scars from tumbling down mountains and
ninety
thousand freckles from sun kisses and
ninety
dreams blossomed into gardens
but despite the minutes of my
feet on the earth I know that
each second
ninety
million nerve endings are firing so that
my lungs can rise again and
I'm holding on like
each second
is my savior so
what if I don't live to be
ninety
but oh god
what if I do?

46

I am woman
I am wonder-filled.

I am a mountain range
speckled with snow
standing strong against
your elements.
I rage like
salt water in a storm,
carrying you
on my back like
bricks but
I am soft enough to
drown you.

I am woman
I am wonder-filled.

47

it's wild how the older you get,
the more you see and experience -
the smaller your mind gets.
it's as though it is afraid of wondering,
afraid of the outcome of curiosity because
it has wandered into fire before.
it hurts that I used to feel so much more;
to be changed by art once and
now my soul is frigid and afraid.
how do I stay malleable and
yet strong against the tenacious heat of reality?
if only my spirit would melt in the hot sun,
liquid gold to be stirred and
always glistening in the movement of being.
but instead brick walls are built around it so
I feel nothing.
I protect myself so much that I am empty and
I ache for this.
is it freedom to feel?
should I live each moment like a meteor,
bright and blazing on a constant current
though I know I will burn out in the end?
these questions haunt me with each burst
of blood from my vessels because
what else matters besides being?
as I slowly decay my spirit rages on with
each breath whispering,
"Be."

48

sometimes I feel like
I could just dig into my skin
and slowly peel it back until
my true form emerges
like this shell of flesh is a
straight jacket holding me
until I go numb from fighting it
like my heartbeat could just
shatter my frame if it felt like it
my fragile corpse swaying
in the wind and my tiny soul
flickers like a flame at
the end of a burned match.
sometimes I feel like
minutes are just the
grains of dirt that fill the
hole you're buried in.
sometimes I feel like
my feelings could be
the sickness or
the cure and what
kills me is that I'll
never know the
difference

49

if I die young
don't weep for me.
I have lived
a life overflowing.
I have seen the world
I have known sweet souls
I have known love
sweeter than the
summer sun.

if I die young
don't bury me
in a cemetery.
I am no longer here so
turn my body into
a tree of life.
you can sit beneath the shade,
breathe deeper as its offspring
keep the time of the seasons
of your own life and remember -

life is precious
life is beautiful
life is yours.

50

this heart is tiny and timid but
its beat makes the floors shake and the
drums in your ears pulse and you
feel the blood flowing
quickly through your veins and you
put your hand to your chest because
god, life is a cobweb in the wind
and this beating is the only thing
keeping your feet on the ground so
don't grab onto the clouds but
watch them with wonder as your
eyelids flutter with
the shaking leaves and let your soul
grow into the earth like roots
so the thumping in your chest will feel
more like fireworks than a
firing squad and I promise
there is healing where the hurt was
hope where the heart broke and
every day on this side of the earth is
worth it

51

we held hands in the sun walking through the streets I was raised in. I made a home for you in a quiet corner of my heart. I filled it with colorful tapestries, candles that smell like innocence, and music that floats like a cool breeze through you. we walked on the moon and the glow beneath us ignited courage in our hearts. the stars covered us in sparkling beauty, a gentle blanket in a cold reality. we laid our bodies on the earth while the sky spilled autumn leaves around us. there was no separation between our souls and creation, a colorful curiosity stirring inside of us. the pouring rain engulfed us as we sat motionless. the cleansing water told us we were free. our spirits lifted and danced with the rain that day and we knew. without saying words we always know. hearts like ours are soft like clay but bright as diamonds. I made a home for you in a quiet corner of my heart. this home is safe and soft, a nest for you to rest. stay as long as you need.

there's this
beating in my chest
that belonged to you
as the leaves were born on barren branches
your name bloomed within me and
created a home there
you were a cherry blossom
and I inhaled your scent like
a healing breath
I saw the sky alive in your eyes and felt
my heart like a hummingbird
and without warning
your petals wilted and fell around me
leaving me with a withered memory
a hope so temporary and every day
I see the tree you lived on that is now
flowerless but I know like spring
love will always return
it will heal this heart in pieces like petals
and the promise of cherry blossoms
makes me whole
as I call this
beating in my chest
my own

53

I've lost discernment between dream and reality.
I saw your back facing me but
maybe I didn't.
you turned to face me and your eyes
told me the story of your emptiness.
you kissed my cheek and
walked over the edge of the cliff.

I saw my heart breaking before me but
maybe I didn't.
It was beating, beating, beating
to the rhythm of our song and
I thought I smelled your scent.
tear-stained pillows are all that
remain from that damp, warm night.
I can barely remember the shape of your
ears or the texture of your hands but
your voice sings a painful melody in my ears.

I saw an old piano in a forgotten room but
maybe I didn't.
a woman I saw at the train station appeared and
sat at the bench.
she laid her head on the keys in defeat.
the chords moan and split
playing the song of her heartache.

I've lost discernment between dream and reality.
I'm seeing myself now but
maybe I'm not.
I walk toward the woman and whisper in her
ear:

the sun rises and falls
like your lungs in perfect harmony.
five senses,
four limbs,
three freckles in constellation,
two eyes and
one heart sending blood in circulation
like the earth around the sun.
remember:
"I am alive."

54

broken
blind
bleeding
but still
feeling
and I will wait
patiently for
spring to
save me

55

when I wrote down those words
black ink cutting through
clean paper
pen piercing the
snowy page
I was thinking of you.
when I took that photo
my plum lips curled like twine tied
them to the secrets twirled in
my hair and
I was thinking of you.
when my sharp inhale caught me
with my fingers
covering my gaping lips
as the sun dripped down the sky like
a glowing pink popsicle
I was thinking of you.
and if you must know
as I lift my chest
inhaling another moment into my
brief existence
I lick my lips and
lock my eyelids and as
each little flutter of being
goes by
I am thinking of you.

our love is
like the crescent moon
carrying me in
its craters and
cutting me with
its edges
breaking me at
the bow and
singing me to sleep at
the stern we
sway with the
stars in the
milky night
and melt when
morning
comes

57

a happy poem:
I forget.

58

break the beat
taste the scream rising
from your toes and
fluttering in your lungs like
a magician's dove appearing from
darkness

flicker and wave
let the heat of life devour you
melting like wax
as a beautiful
fiery
avalanche

colorful courage
flowers flow through your veins
and your spirit stretches
and groans like the
trees in a windstorm

feel it all
orange and white
burn your skin
life is full of you
and the stars burn
bright and blazing
even in the
darkest blue

59

she unfolds before you like
pages in your favorite
book like
a blazing rose in spring
and you ache for her
longing to discover
the rhythm in her breath
the pattern her eyelashes flutter as
they send chills through your skin like
ocean waves and you gaze
at her spirit
as it sparkles like
stars in the velvet night

60

I am free
despite what my mind tells me
oxygen flows like a gentle breeze
through mountain top trees
and my limbs are strong like
giant pines
full of life and seeping the sap of
righteousness
fighting through the seasons
endless patience and
silent wisdom
I am free
despite what you tell me
my heart stomps through
muddy trenches
and the rain floods my veins
and no one
can take
my freedom
from me

BURN THIS

I made this for you
this kindling
this ink pounded into paper
these recycled stories
I made this for you
for when the
ache is too much
for when the
emptiness is eating you
for when your
voice can't carry you
for when you feel
that you're stranded
dark and alone
I made this for you
so douse it
with gasoline
let it light like
a lantern like
a warm welcome like
a blazing cry
in the night
I made this for you
so use it
when you need it
send it up like smoke
into the stars and
you will
be found

PART II

WIND WHISPERING SECRETS FEW HAVE EARS TO HEAR

WIND WHISPERING SECRETS FEW HAVE EARS TO HEAR

it's a
language
only we
know
it's a
frequency
for us
the nocturnal
never-sleeping
silently storming
warriors
with each inhale
we fight
for life
for freedom
for us.
it's a
silent
swearing-in
ceremony
we hear it in
groaning ancient trees
we hear it in
chill winter breeze
and you will
find us finally
free

WORTHY

my body moves
my body heals
my body stretches and shrinks
curls when I need it to
aches as a warning to slow down
propels me in an instant
my body could create new life
my body speaks what words can't
it holds heaven and horrors in
the curves of my shoulders
my body is miraculous
endless nerve endings synapsis
firing electricity pulls me in
this vessel
this momentary
home for my soul
this gift and yet
I hate it
I loathe this shipping container
although it's transporting well
instead of its worth being weighed
in the amount of space
between my thighs
around my arms and the
sterility of my skin
I will choose to weigh it
in the distance it's gone
in the glow it gives off
my body moves
my body heals
and I
am worthy

FIRST

I'll always
love you
I'll never
love with the
same amount of reckless abandon.
the love I have for him now
is woven into me with
clear thread
it's there when I look into
the mirror but I can't
see it
the love I have for you
left a permanent stain
eye-catching and grotesque
it's grown and bled over the years.
I'll always
love you
I'll never
be with you again

THE SCALE

justice
feels like
fog in my
fists
a blinding
force
unmistakable
existence
however
elusive and we
can't determine
can't define
it after all of these
horrifying
harrowing
heedless
years and still we
put ourselves
above the
prisoner

SLEEP, A LONGING

death
rests on my
chest
when it's not
plunging its
bladeless knife
in my belly
it purrs
heavy bearing
down on me
never letting me
forget its
presence
the dark haze
surrounding
suffocates
as it
slowly
spills over me until
I
disappear

SUFFOCATING, LATE JULY

these summer
nights
are swallowing me
like the
dark
unknowable sea
these summer
nights
are far too
dark
for me

Can you feel it?

est-ce que tu le sens?

✕ ⚠ ◢ ⦂

THE WEIGHT OF EMPATHY

when I hear the word 'empath' I feel this grip at my throat this ripping out a half from my whole because I don't think they understand I don't think they can fathom half of the weight or half of the exhaustion or half of the misery

sometimes I want to bang fists into bricks and scream into silence it hurts so much the misery of others. it's so unfair that I could carry all of this along with the weight of my own mortality, the consequences of consciousness, but I bear every burden. I hold his and hold the heaviness of my own.

GLITCH

I wonder
often if
what I'm seeing
is a simulation
adrift from reality
slightly skewed from
what it seems
maybe there's a
glitch in the system
any time I start
to question anything
any time suicide seems
a viable option
it's an error in the programming
I wonder
often if
what we see
isn't at all
what it seems

THIS SICKNESS ASKS

why
why
why
keep on living
when it feels like
suffocating
when it feels like
drowning
when it feels like
you're pulling them
down with you
when it feels like
the chains link on and
on for all eternity and
you're powerless
despite the false sense of
respite that's been
disguised as freedom
when the blinding brightness of
all of the dark empty nothingness
devours you
why
why
why
keep on dying

RELIEF

in the scheme of the
universe and
all of its billions
I am nothing.
I am nothing
and
I am relieved

MAYBE

brutal
burning
empty hollow ghost
my soul is a whisper
within this boarded up
cage I'm
shaken to the core
empty and riddled with
rage I'm
unable to carry the
weight
any longer
but maybe
there's someone
stronger than me
to share this
unbearable
burden
to throw me a
life-raft
in this stormy sea

My dearest Bambi,

The words 'I miss you' will never do justice to the aching
pits, the dark craters of longing spread across my soul,
the heaviness of your laughter being but a memory. The
first moment upon waking, dim light leaking through my
heavy lids, I expect to see you next to me. You would
sleep earlier and later than I, so I got the deep joy
of watching your pure rest beside me. So peaceful, the
vessel which carries your heart - and mine - one. I
fight with the fact that this isn't a dream. That they
made me leave you . That they took my joy.

I think of you always. The moment I see your smile will
be the moment my heart is whole again. Until then, my love.

Love always,

Binx

FOCUS

so do we
shift the lenses on
the moments when
we're victims when
injustice wins?
so do we
call off the dogs
once one thing seems
to be going well
or do we continue
shining a light
on the wrong?
I don't want to
be one to
focus only
on the lowness.
people can always
carry heavier
so what can I
do for them?

UNCOVERED

I don't know if you know
how soft I am
how my skin is prone
to sunburns to
scratch marks to
the deep scars of
cold words
I don't know if you know
how weak I am
I've never been given
protection from the
harsh wind from the
smoke and mirrors
that they call
sin and
I don't know if I'll ever know
who,
in the end,
wins

TO BARE

anxiety
pulls at the
thread that
holds you
together you
feel it unraveling
this painful
separation
from yourself
this frightening
freedom of
overwhelming thought
letting the light in where
it hasn't been before
blinding and burning it's
awakening senses
that are better kept
sleeping it's
grotesque in its
reality not hiding
like the others just
baring boney
teeth there's
nothing to hide
when
anxiety
opens up the autopsy
of what's really
inside

A SEASON'S CHANGE, ANOTHER

I think the only thing that hurts worse than death is birth. the passage of time is a slow ache, memories are hot to the touch. leaving the past behind is a heartbreak, facing the unknown, yet another lonely day only to burn again. remembering and forgetting are a similar fire. cover me in gasoline.

WITHIN

salvation
seduces me
with a slithering
tongue it
tells me to
trust to
take the
path
without
thorns
but I
stumble
in each
and I
have only
splinters after
searching with
fingernails
and faith
and I
hold onto
my own strength
rooting tall as
a tree
knowing that
only I
can
save me

they'll never know

what we know

CHESHIRE

it can be truly overwhelming
you know
all the lives we're not living
all the paths we're not taking
and the suffocating reality
of the ticking clock
and its irreversible motion
ever forward we
must move unyieldingly
facing life with unbroken breath
or we may miss a moment
in the ice rink of living because
you will slip any second now and it's
over
the lights go black and you are
gone
so how do you possibly accept this
tyranny of time
so vast and yet so inexplicably
irreversible and you are at its whim;
a bet I am unwilling to take
a stake so high I can't possibly fathom
a fully lit life so
let's take every path for
if you don't know where you're going,
"then," said the cat,
"it doesn't matter."

AN ARTIST

it must be
miserable
having a
mind
like that

SPARK

like tiny dust particles
reflecting in the morning light
our lives are a glimmer
in time
caught by the eye of the
universe for just an instant
a freckle in the eye of a
homeless man clinking change in a
bucket we are unnoticed and overall
unnecessary to the world spinning
around the sun more times
than you'll blink your eyes
and if that doesn't terrify you
nothing will

SICK

disease-ridden
writers
wreaking havoc
on your
wildest dreams
we sicken the
weak
with our
open minded
careful
cautious
cruelty
I'm never who
they hoped
I'd be when they
first meet me
I'm never what
they think
I'll become
if only they could
cure me

NEW

making up for lost time
creating and recreating
shedding skin and
exhaling the dust of life
and rising with the sun
forget the darkness like a dream
cling with clenched fists
to the light

they'll never know

what we know

START

gold velvet on the skin
soft edges sinking in
and the dim lighting fills
your lungs and your soul
is full of Egyptian cotton
smooth silk seeps into your pores
and as the smoke rises to heaven
your fears dissolve and you are
one with the sea foam salty breeze
abandon anxiety and ditch depression
as you inhale deeply and hear
the crackling fire
singeing your sadness
burning your burdens to the ground
as each vessel brims boldly
with a bright elation you didn't
know existed glowing off of you.
every morning
is a new season
and you
are a new you.

ONE WITH THE CLOUDS

melt into the earth
sea foam over rocks
swallow and exhale
feel free and one
with the clouds
feel your fingertips brush
the Galaxy
and tears bubbling over
volcanic explosion
of purpose
your heart beats with the
stampedes in the west
you are both mother and child
the Stars spell out your name
and you are
here
and you are
whole

LIGHT

do you remember
your first breath and
oh god
will you remember
your last?

MY HAND

this is for when you crave the burn
like swallowing
singes your insides like
black coals with orange outlines
like it hurts until
it can't anymore until
scars cover your skin like scales as
a dark armor for the fire.
this is for when you crave the burn
like a raging river
runs through your veins
pulling you like claws
into the grave but
you need it
more than breathing
more than bleeding
because hurting is healing.
this is for when you crave the burn
when all you want
is to let the sorrow
swallow you please
take this like a life raft
and please
never let it go.

and please
let me die by
the fire
of life

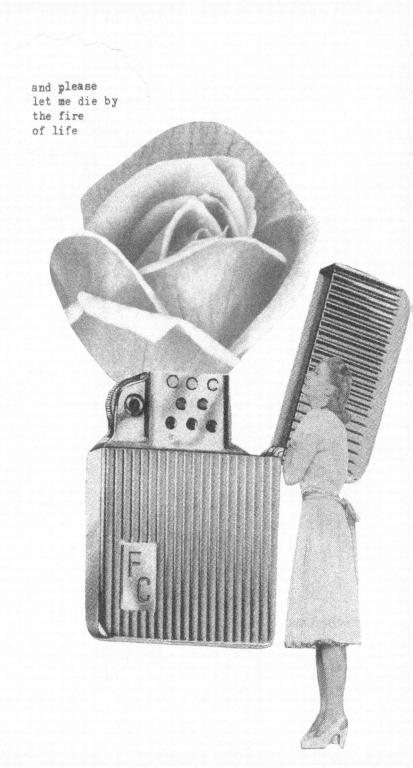

and my heart aches for him because

he, like me,
will never be free

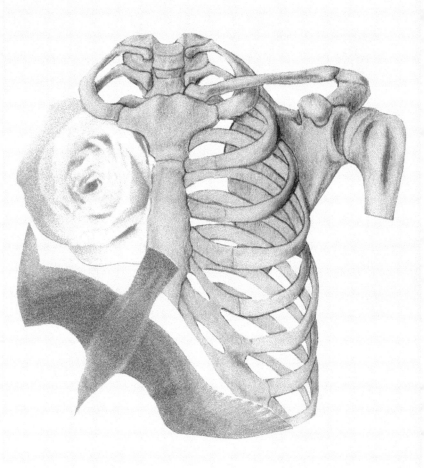

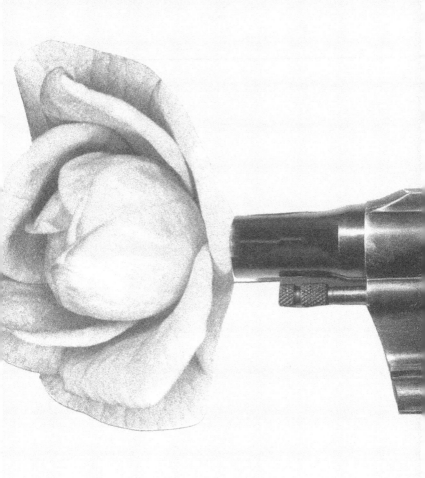

so the thumping in your chest will feel
more like fireworks than a
firing squad

a happy poem:
I forget

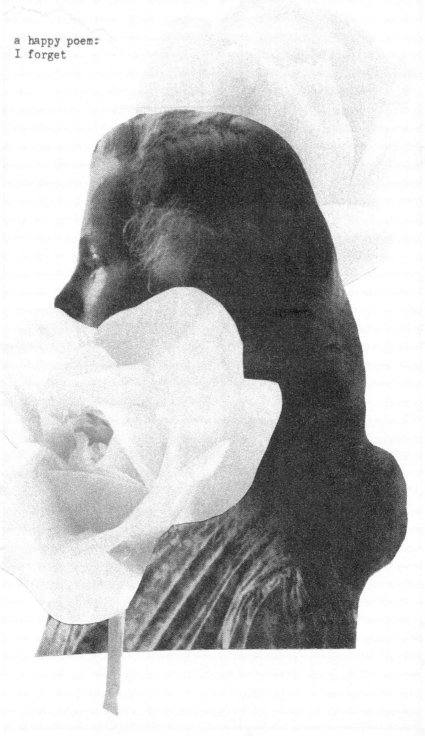

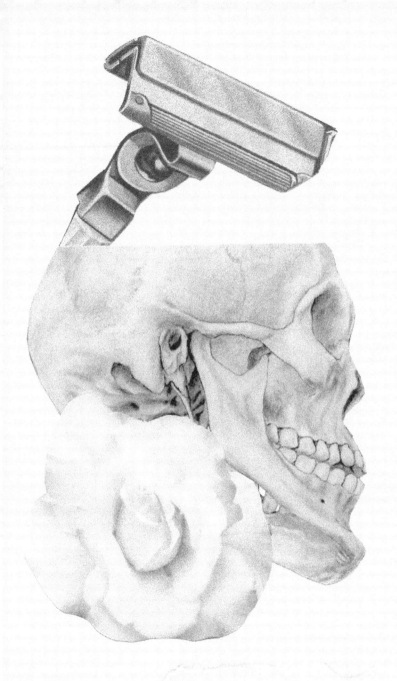

I am free
despite what my mind tells me

so how do you possibly accept this
tyranny of time

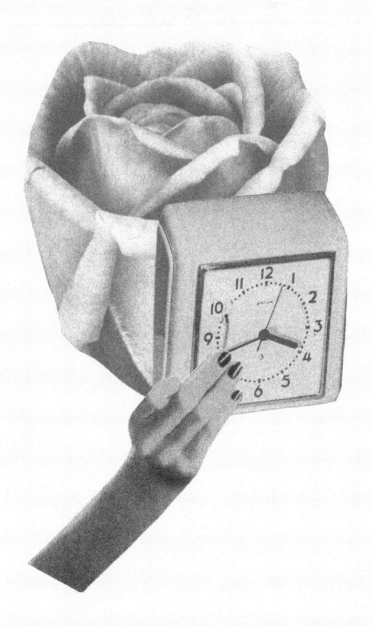

PART III

THE MOODS OF DEEPEST ROOTS

THE MOODS OF DEEPEST ROOTS

I close my eyes and
I see my limbs
crawling outward and
inward they sprawl
to the sky and they
bury in the earth
my veins winding around
the roots
all
the
way
down to the earth's core
and for a moment
we are one
and for a moment
I am free
and for a moment
I am truly Me

BEFORE SPRING

head splits
and aches and bleeds
and sorrow seeps out of
my pores despite
my posture
despite my smile
and my white teeth
my heart ebbs and flows
like the tide scraping rocks
and I feel it all
and you know all that I
know and it's okay
to hurt and to
cry and to crack
and the red spills out and
we stand and we smile and
we break and
it's going to be,
it has to be,
beautiful
in the end

WOUNDED

in those quiet
moments before
sleep
do you think of
me?
I swear I feel your skin
on mine and we're
swaying
in and out like
the tide
a warm whisper in
my ear and
suddenly you're
here wrapped
around me like a
bandage and it
couldn't be more
fitting

FROZEN

I'm thawed when
the heat of your breath
on my neck
brings me back to life
your whisper
stings my ear and I'm
suddenly a spark
my eyes alive
for you
devouring every piece
of you
and I burn until I'm
holy
ashes
all around

DISTANCE

last night
I dreamt of you
it felt like cool
water flowing through
my caves and then
I woke up
hot and humbled
drowning in
daylight and the
distance between
my dream and
you feels like
galaxies like
landmine-filled
fields and
I can't decide
whether or not
it's worth the
journey

BALANCE

you are the shadows in
the moon that make me feel
small but beautiful
and you are the weeds in
the garden that
drive me crazy but still
remind of summer and warmth
and I'll never get around you because
you are the clouds that block
the sunlight saving me from
the burn but also
bringing rain and
it's the balance
that keeps me sane

are you still here?

etes-vous toujours la?

STAINED

they'll never know
the words
whispered in the
dark under the
summer moon and
they'll never know
the music
that plays when
I think of you
secrets weave
a tangled web
between us and
I can't quite seem
to get your scent
out of my
soul

STOLEN SENSES

it's been
one year but
god your scent still
sets my skin on fire
like dry grass in august and
god I need you
like the rain because
my fingers feel empty without yours and
the air seems too thin without your breath
so please just please
don't forget me because
god it hurts to feel
so little and
everything
all at once

KNOW

you were born from the universe
close your eyes and see the galaxy
open them and watch the stardust dance
milky moons wash over you
moss makes up your insides and
you bleed lava
feel the burn of change on your flesh
groan with the ancient trees and
know, if only,
this:
your spirit is spectacular

ARISE

the mattress beneath her
creaks under the pressure
she closes her eyes and cracks
each knuckle one by one
desperately trying to feel she
slows her breathing and
closes her eyes
lashes intertwine and
all is dark as the
silence screams
when will it end? or more accurately,
when will it begin?
her eyelids lift with her body
off of this old mattress in this old house
placing her feet on the ground her
soul demands:
arise

FORGETTING

I remind myself to breathe.

I'm watching an old film and an elderly woman has two lines and all I can think is how she is no longer alive.

and my heartbeat is louder in my ears now.

I lie here on this chaise covered in a blanket with my cat and I watch her breathe in and out. her rib cage raising and falling and a sweet whimper as she stretches. I always notice the temporary aspects of existence.

I'll hear his heartbeat when I lay on his chest and be consumed with the cardiac mortality. this beating will end one of these days. will it be mine or his first? we're all responsible for one another. it's all so fragile.

and my heartbeat is louder in my ears now.

sometimes I just want to live through a day and forget that I'm living. sometimes I just want to live through a day and forget that I'm dying.

I remind myself to breathe.

My dear Binx,

I remember the time you bit my cheek. We were hanging
out with your friends on a clear summer night. I didn't
know you well then. Your arm hung loose around my shoulders,
but I felt safe, I felt yours. Your laughter shook the
fire from the tiki torches as you threw your empty beer
can in the pool. I didn't say much that night. Your smile
made it hard to breathe, the way your gaze locked into
mine, and your eyes. They crippled me. All I could do
was smile in a way that turned my cheeks into juicy peaches
and you took a bite. I never really got to know your friends.
I didn't need to. The only people that existed then were
you and me. I'll never forget how I felt that night, like
a flower in full bloom. I'll never forget your summer
skin in the moonlight.

I ache for you. I'll be here waiting.

Forever,

Bam bi

HEAT

one day
two years
tight chest
weary eyes
time flies and
drags like a broken leg
aching and suffering
longing for freedom
breaking the chains of
time and space
crossing the border
of the universe
to float like a star
glowing like warm
coals in a raging fire

EVERYTHING

some days
i
don't exist
my body moves me
muscles bend and stretch
my lungs expand and
i
go on
trees and leaves and
people spin around me and
i
act and
i
breathe
and
i
survive
but
i
am not here
i
function and
i
forget that
i
still
am everything

FINITE

dark black
surrounds as I count down
the moments left of today
until tomorrow becomes today
and we continue holding our breath
until we're one with the sky
blue in the face won't get us
to the place we long for most
tomorrow does not exist
we only have a second to do
infinite things
to be everywhere and everyone
just hold on like roots in a storm
breathe life into your lungs
fresh release
march
forward
and be.

TRYING

your velvet night
sky soul
slips through my
fingers, and
your moonbeam
madness is
always just out
of reach

FEBRUARY 96

dead trees stretch
their arms toward heaven
begging for the light to
eat them up
for their weary limbs
release
for the sweet embrace
of life and leaves
nourishing like green
tear drops cleansing

IN CASE YOU WERE WONDERING

depression is like trying to roll up a hill

while the rocks are rolling down.

ABSENCE

it's the shape of
your hands that
haunts me the
tiny crevices kept
me safe and I made
my home in
the lines that sway
in such a way that only
you could create
a safe circular
space that I seemed
to fit more
comfortably than
in my own
skin

FEMININE

just
because
I'm soft
doesn't mean
you can
touch me

HIDDEN

maybe I see you
like a bud on a branch
bright green
young and gleaming in
the winter sun
while the branches
still scream against
the blinding snow and
maybe I see you
crawling out of the
cold ground the
first fern that
fought for life,
held out for warmth and
you have no idea how
strong your spirit is

AFTER

nomad heart
wandering wonderful life
floating an inch off the ground
rooted nowhere and knowing
nothing of Home
this land that birthed
us doesn't even know us
doesn't want to know
just dies a slow and painful
death and this earth
this soil this air
is nothing compared
to the glittering everything that
is promised to us
the warm glow of contentment
knowing nothing of ache or want
but knowing full
and being fully known

PART IV

CURIOSITIES CALLED OUT FROM LEAGUES UNDER THE SEA

CURIOSITIES CALLED OUT FROM
LEAGUES UNDER THE SEA

I want to dip into
divinity
like liquid quartz crystal
both covering
and uncovering
carrying light
calm and cool
powerful like a
pink sky
soaks you
baptizing
in boldness
calling out all
curiosities and
curing the
famine
that is
humanity.

61

when I dive
to my depths it's
a slow motion hurricane
galaxies orbiting
tidal waves
crash and
clear
over and
over
stars spin bright and
I'll never have both
feet on the ground but
give me the deep,
I'd rather drown.

62

white flakes falling
ashes in the dark
the black
streets glow under the
warm lamps and I
fight to find the beauty
in the crisp clean air
in the snow floating
by as light as a feather
but all I can think is
'this is dying weather'

63

I just
want to know
why
planes will
fall out of the sky
while carrying
a father to visit his
daughter for her
first chemotherapy
treatment and
why
are some children
gone before they knew
they were here and
why
have I been granted even
one more day
of open eyes and
oxygen to breathe when there are
mothers whose sons were
shipped away
in the name of being brave
and they didn't even
get to say their
last
goodbye

64

I'm so sorry that
when you look into my eyes
you feel the heaviness of storm clouds and
I'm so sorry that
I'm so afraid of everything that
you have to carry me over every rock and
I'm so sorry that
the weight of my burdens fill up your space
so that you can barely breathe because
all I want is to set you free
from the prison that is
me

65

the train
it chews through
the tracks
near my house and I
hear it
late at night it
yells louder than
he does
louder than
the music I put in my ears
so I can't pretend
it's not there
so I can't pretend
I'm not there
and
I hate it.
the train
it screams and
I wish
I could
too.

66

I feel as though I'm a tower, tall and alone and
there's a trench around me,
filled with rushing water with no bridge across it.
I'm trapped inside myself and
I only feel safe feeling nothing at all.
the weeds are growing higher and I'm hiding
behind them.
if you're looking for me,
I'll be here
holding on behind the madness.

67

my soul is like sand. warm and soft and soothing you dig in and you mold it with your hands, rolling and turning and pushing and pulling. you make it yours and I let you. you are both everything and nothing next to it. these tiny grains, they worship you. you are infinite in front of them. but then they come together and they are endless and they carry you. I feel each grain of my soul groaning on with every creature that I encounter. I am made from mountains and I feel everything and I fear failing you. I don't know how many more castles I can become only to be swallowed by the sea. I don't know how to be without you touching me.

68

the glistening ends of
wolves' teeth
beckon me
the sharp daggers and
bloodthirsty eyes
call me by name
the howling cry of
hunger and I'm the
taste it craves and
I can't seem to
look away

69

he,
like poison,
will
only kiss to
kill

why are you?

pourquoi es-tu?

70

after years of feet on earth's ground does there come a time when all you ever do is cope? blinking breathing blowing out candles. it's not living anymore, it's surviving. with each step forward you're just trying to dig out of a hole you fell in years ago. how do you feel like you're floating? not striving not swimming but being pulled gently in a calm current, sun sparkling on chilled blue ripples beside you. how do you keep from falling? as each day passes the ground beneath you loosens and you know the ledge is near, will you ever see it coming?

71

do you remember
that time when
you said 'always'
like it was chocolate
melted in your mouth
a moving moment
left on your lips
until it trickled
off your tongue
and the letters
left you along with
the meaning along with
any kind of commitment
or careful comment and
I don't know
if you realize
the way that word
covered me like a blanket
that I didn't know would
soon suffocate

72

today I felt my skin
like it was sand in
a windstorm
stirring in the
strength of the
elements and I
lost control
long ago
my body
moves with
earth's sorrow
weeps with
widows and
breaks as the
days simmer
shrinking slowly
spilling through the
sand timer there
is always
an end

73

I welcome death
every
dark ditch
every
dam
calling me
down
deeper
into the dark
I feel the hands
around my neck
tighten each moment and
I let them
as I shiver with the
cold black
coils wrapped around me
pulling me
under and
taking me
home

74

to be truthful
I make it
my mission to
quiet or to
listen to the
empathy
one or the
other extreme
I'm either
giving all of me
or
I'm dying to
hide for
only a moment
it feels like it could
kill me and
to be truthful
it would be
welcome

75

what if the
world was under
water and we didn't
know it
we're actually just small particles
clinging to another
organism
surviving off of its
nutrients and we're
leeches
floating through space sucking
the life out of our home
and what if this
is reality

76

I take life slow
so I can savor
each flavor
becoming familiar
with the bitter
and the sweet and
finding a beautiful
balance of each.
I take the long way home
so I can feel
each street
between my teeth
biting down
on ripe cherry
sunset skies
feeling every cool breeze
fill me and
tasting the trees
knowing we share the
same roots and
knowing that where
we came from is where
we are going

77

it's strange isn't it
how emptiness can
consume you
this hollow
hungry beast
reaches through you
filling every corner
and crevice
and there's
nowhere to hide so
you do all you can
and pray
oh god
you pray
to no longer be alive but
remember
spring always
comes after
winter's gloom
the flowers
are there just
waiting for
you to bloom

78

sometimes I wonder
if I'm made up of more
goodbyes
than
hellos.
all the pin pricks
and knee-scrape scars
compile to
complete the version
of me that
I see in the mirror
while I still seem
to be unfamiliar
with my own chemicals,
with the person
you left that
cold night,
hot breath like smoke in
the air as I turned
to ash.
sometimes I wonder
if I'm made up of more
goodbyes
than
hellos
and sometimes I wonder
who I would be if
you had never uttered
either
weary
word
to me

My sweet Bambi,

I know I just wrote you, but I'm missing you and I would
rather be talking to you than anything else. I'm sitting
alone at a tiny bistro table on a sun-soaked Puerto Rican
boulevard. The weather is perfect today. Bright blue with
small clouds, peaceful, like the world was just born.

Taking breaks from writing to pick up my cigarette and
take a drag, lifting my glass of red wine with my left hand
and washing down the weight of the world. I pause my music
to hear the birds chirp for a moment and to breathe in
the present. Press play to return to Beethoven's Sonata
No. 14 "Moonlight" in C-Sharp Minor. I have such a pleasant
relationship with melancholy. Self-destructive behaviors
dance alongside this golden afternoon and I feel okay.

Open my Zippo lighter, the black one with a crescent moon
above mountains, to light my second, but the flame never
came. I've moved on to Chopin and I'm not quite sure why
I'm still writing. I'm distracted by the shadows of flickering
leaves, and what I wouldn't do to be one of them.

And maybe I am// My existence is brief and overall unextra-
ordinary. Contributing to a greater purpose, releasing
oxygen into the eco-system, providing shade for plants
to live under, for creatures to live and breathe among.

Anyway, I don't know why I'm still writing. Remember that
in every small moment I am thinking of you. I'm going
to go get another lighter and another glass of Merlot .
Take care, My Sweet.

Love always,
Binx

79

I often wonder
if I'm a ghost.
a ghoulish
resemblance of
someone who once
was,
a past tense,
a vessel
only meant to carry
this spirit from
one life to the
next and maybe
this can explain
the emptiness maybe
this can explain
the fear of
unfulfillment because
deep down I know
it's not for me.
I am flesh and
I am bones but will
I ever really
be me?

80

I don't
know
if I believe
anymore
in the whisper
in the willows
bending being
burden-bearing
anything
or that
everything
has to mean
something
and even though
freedom from feeling
is healing
I can't
help but burn in
my wholly
hell-less existence
I don't
know
anymore
and the sorrow
swells like a holy
spirit engulfing in
the flames of
infinite endless
meaningless burning
anything
and
I can't

figure out what to
do now that
I don't

81

humanity
is constant
hunger
a curse of an
inextinguishable
curiosity,
desires with no
words to describe them
fears for which there
is no escape and
here we are
fighting for it
anyway

this sleepy
slow
suicide
lazy
lonely and
leave me
because I'm
heavy
empty
and I have a
contagious
sickness so
save yourself
leave me to
rest in
this quiet
frightening
Forever

83

another night of no sleep and swirling words and snap-shots and last night's wild romance. my favorite time of year is when it stays warm at night. it's unbearably hot in the daytime and we're all wandering through the same delirium. there's this haze around everything, it's so bright that you forget how sharp the edges are.

84

we all
carry the weight
of our ancestors
the burdens they
bore the misery
mounted upon them
and injustice
incapacitates the
inferior
the weaker
skin tone
the lesser sex
the invalid
birthplace.
we are more than
our appearance
we are
carrying the yolk
of slavery to our
heritage but
what they
wish was wrong
what they
work to
make us forget
is that
we are strong

85

can you hold
your whole
life in
your hands?
touch the
time spent with
special
someones,
feel the
failures and
absorb the
absences,
waking up
to each
wearily
wonderful
moment
we all have
a heaviness
not all are
strong enough
to hold

86

when
will I be
wrung out?
I've absorbed
every single
sadness like a
sponge,
spilling over
because the
weight of the
world is
too much.
it's heavy, the
heartache of every
human you come
in contact with.
it's hard not to
bear the
burden of every
being in front of you.
so what do I do
when it hurts to
hold on for
everyone else?
I've absorbed
too much of this
murky life
when
will I be
wrung out?

87

sometimes I
wish I lived my life
in black and white
a scale of
grey
dancing through each
day
without the
weight of
shades of blues
and the ways the
green or its lack
can break you

are
you
here?

San Juan, Puerto Rico

88

not dead but
not quite
alive either
numb and
not sure how
to hope anymore how
to hold onto
reality it's
a severed
system
we're fully
aware
in this
walking
waking and
never-ending
nightmare

89

you are the
marrow in my bones
the molecules
that make up
my humanness
my temporary
time capsule
completed by your
essence
years have tied us
together
tears and laughter
weeping and worries
shared are the thread
through us and it
hurts to share a body
but I'm glad
it's with you

90

Call me out from
Under the heavy hell of
Reality, reel me in
Slowly to the shore of
Eternity, free to breathe the fresh air of
Death

91

I ask the universe,
"what is my worth?"
my worries
define me
my fears
fill me and seem
to be entwined
with my desires
dancing to a
melancholy song
I ask the universe,
"what is my worth?"
I am a tangled web
made of mischief and
mistakes
broken dreams and
empty promises
hollowed out
I ask the universe,
"what is my worth?"
every shattered piece
of me longs
to know,
and all I hear in response is
an echo

92

the sky has just finished weeping
it seems to be breathing heavily
bearing the burden of endless
galaxies, the earth's elements
come through as unwelcome visitors
and despite all of this
it remains beautiful
it remains strong
it remains

93

I want
to be wild
to be free
wobbling on the edge of
ecstasy and misery
dancing between
fear and freedom
inhaling every wet ounce
of existence
I can't stay still
long enough to be
satiated so
I am always thirsty
longing
to lose
desperate
to defeat
the hungry beast
inside of me
do you know it?
that gruesome creature
devouring contentment
painting a portrait of you
grotesque enough
to make you believe that
to be wild is
to be free

94

fear and
pleasure are
not far from
each other.
do I
dread death or
do I
desire death because
I dig deep in the depths of the
unknown
swimming further into black ocean
hoping to cure
my eternal
never-ending
dehydration

95

fire-sword swallower
my freak show
I feel it ripping
though my throat down
to my soul and then
the fire fills me from
my veins
to my feet
and it's strangely
freeing
burning away my
outer layer
it's a poisonous drink but
it takes me higher
and
I don't know how to live
without this fire

96

hell is
not as far as you think
it's jagged branches and
barbed wire fences
it's boards nailed into buildings
white crosses
where there should
be headstones
hell is
saying goodbye before
you would ever choose to
it's this insatiable hunger
for any sense of hope
in all of this isolation
it's a world under ice with only
fingernails to scrape
hell is
here
and death
I fear
will be no escape

fish or catcher

we bleed the same

if poetry
is purity
empathy
a form of
expression
misery a
meaning in this
malicious
existence
I'll never have
enough
my cup will overflow
and then I know
I will need more
because I'm
bleeding out and I'm
feeling nothing
so I'll take what I can get
fire and fuel
aren't fears anymore
but instead I'm afraid of
numbness of
a world
where poetry
is punitive
purpose
is malignant I'm
afraid it's too
hard to find
a reason why
I should stay alive

98

'can you hear me?'
I'm always pleading and
I don't know how
to be heard
anymore
my screams
are just hot
breath evaporating
my molecules
dissolving and
no one seems to see the
disintegration the
degradation the
true disillusion of
a time when
my voice seemed to
mean something
my words more than
mere smoke
mere mirrors
I don't know how
to be heard
anymore
are you listening?
am I even speaking?
maybe it's just a mist
in the void or
maybe it's just missed
behind the noise as
I swallow my sorrow
I can hardly breathe it's
a cough and it's

blood and
I choke
'can you hear me?'

can art only
come from
melancholy?
or does
creation ever
come from
a place of
peace of
pure flowing
streams instead
or furious
rivers over
rocks
it's broken
breath between
sobs between
goodbyes I
find it hard to
believe that art can
come from
anything other than
the deepest aching
burrowing burying
masochistic misery
please free me from
this dark black
reality

100

I am suspended
my feet are
off the ground but
I'm not quite
in the clouds
I am stranded
a dreamer with an
inextinguishable fire
always passionate
always perplexed
I am suffocating
my feet are
flailing hoping to feel
ground beneath them as
I grip the rope at
my throat but maybe
I am soaring
if I only lift my
weary wings
above my
heavy head
"have hope"
they said
before I leapt
eyes tight shut
where will I end up?
soaring
in the blue
or strangled
in the noose?

101

I am truly curious
about the life of a
human who feels light an
existence which doesn't
nauseate at all hours the
sleep one would have
having no deep-
rooted darkness
I am truly fascinated
by the surface-dwelling
decades of deliberate
delusionists
how do they do it
how do they swallow back
the retching ugly
reality
it's hideous and I
can't hold it and
I am truly dying
because I'm alone
amongst the empty
mannequins
amongst the floating
fools
I am truly aching
for an unquenchable longing
for the eternal
and gasping
relief
from this leeching life but
there are humans who don't hurt
like this and while

it breaks me to my core
I step back and with
weary wonder
I am truly curious

102

imagine
going through life
rarely thinking
about the enormous
weight of existence
and the beautiful
thin thread of mortality
and forgetting the
finiteness of it all.

I can't.

103

motions
follow
emotions
breathing
precedes
being
I hold every
hallowed moment in
my holy hands
I carry every
hollow human in
my heavy heart
my thoughts they
travel to you they
wander wearily
in your shadow
I wallow
in this sorrow and
I wonder if
I follow the blue
the deep dark hue
or am
I just
desperate to
be free from you

104

why am I
enamored
with darkness
with death
with the immeasurable
length of the universe
with the unexplorable
depths of the ocean
I'm drawn to the
delightful dark of
delirium to the
dehydration of
deception to the
hallucinations of
holiness
why am I
deceived to
believe that
being wounded is
worth more than
being cured and
why am I
covered in cuts so that
the burn of the
salty tide hurts instead
of heals I'll
never understand
what it would
be like to
finally
feel real

105

I find it
fascinating how
smoke and air
dance it's
another language
an other-worldly
whisper
the way they curl
into each other
and slowly
melt into one
this secret language
rapid in its
storytelling
beautiful remnants of
a devoured being
the gift of death
spinning softly
into eternity

fish or catcher

we bleed the same

106

if only I could be
invincible and
indestructible
instead of
insecure and
inadequate
if only I could be
you
instead of
me
the one
walking away
the one
holding my
heart in your
hands
if only I could be
unbroken or
unforgotten
if only I could be
you
if only I could be
free

107

am I going to miss this sadness?

I'm waning with the sun
and each sleep is teasing an
eternal peace
and this question is eating me
I feel
every
fiber of this
futile finite
existence and
every
ounce of
misery of
everyone but
what keeps me awake
is the gnawing ache
the constant question
I'll always ask is

am I going to miss this sadness?

it's become a home
a way to finally know
my place in
this space
I feel
forward as
I would in the dark
delicately touching
cautiously clutching
fearful and never

truly free
I don't know what
healing would
really be
and if you've
been to
hell before please
help me
hold my hand
and please
answer my only question
amongst all of the madness,

am I going to miss this sadness?

108

I'm so
sorry
I'm so
sick
over the
injustice
over the
imbalance and
I feel
oh god
I feel
it all and
I'm so
sorry
please
please
grip my hand
and know
I'm here and
I feel
as much as I'm allowed
I feel
an ounce of what
you feel
so please know
you're safe with
me
I'll walk into
this war
unwaveringly
with
you

109

I hear
oceans in
my ear
without sea
shell against
I hear
waves and
caves smashing
water only
closed eyes and
sea foam is holding
heavy in my mind
sometimes I
close my eyes and
it's easier to
picture
the sea in
my ear
rather than
the screams
rather than
my heavy heart
hostage
beating
beating
beating
I hear

110

you are the salt to my sea
water to my clouds
filling me until overflow
you are the green to my leaves and
you are brighter when
I'm watered
we cannot exist
apart from each other
and I can't tell if this is
a blessing or
a curse

111

what if I was
beautiful
a sight
tired eyes long to
look upon
a siren
calling on
sorrowful sailors
a sepulcher
what if when I looked
in the mirror I
actually saw
me
instead of a ghostly
silhouette
what if I was

112

we were doomed from the start
our love was a dance and we
could never keep our rhythm
we stepped on toes and
pushed and pulled but
it was our first dance
with each other
with anyone
it was special because
it was new
it was perfect because
it was you.
we were doomed from the start
we were different in every way except
that we loved each other except
when we didn't
or so you told me that
one night in the snow
in your car you told me
you didn't want to be with me
but we both knew you did
you worshipped me and
you still do
pure and holy in my
pedestal you
placed me in
and you
remain as a chronic ache
a boot at my throat when I
think of you
I hate you so much and
I don't at all and

I miss our
messy dance
even though I know
it was never meant to be
you'll always have the
deepest part of me

113

I closed
my eyes and
I memorized
you.
I took my fingertips to
your cheekbones and
I felt
your forehead and
grazed over
your nose and
I followed
the lines of
your lips and
as thumbs gripped your
jawbones
I kissed
you and
after all this time
I can
still feel it
I'm there
in my sleep
breathing
your breath
we lied there and
I memorized
you.
I wonder what
you
think when
your hands trace
her.

I wonder if
my ghost
stirs
and if
it hurts
you
the way it will
always hurt
me.
I closed
my eyes and
I see that without
you
I'll finally
fly

114

curator of consciousness
collector of curiosity
call me a dreamer
a wild creature
I can't control where
my spirit sweeps its
paintbrush sometimes it
splatters and stains or
swirls in such a way
to make you forget
if only for a moment
the horrible
the hollow
the hell
of it all I will always be
this wild creature
cultivating an awareness
of this
covalent
captivity
a weakness created
at creation and we're
in this together
the dreamers
the wild creatures
creating colorful chaos

Love Always,
Bing

Davidson Factory Shop

Bill + Rommel

Winter 1927

Niagara Falls

to Pete Hartman

115

moons
move in slow
motion
orbit around
you
sending soft
signals it's a
calming current
this soft light
lifting and learning
you
it's a nightly navigator
these gentle
mobile meteors
taking their time
illuminating and
evolving
highlighting when you're
hidden in the night
hiding when the
sun tells it to but
you
never remember the
endless galaxies the
stars and rings and
unimaginable blues
please never forget that
you
will always be
more than your
moons

116

it's choking
on your favorite meal
being misunderstood
in your fluent language
trying harder
than you ever have
and still failing
we all fall
short of the
glory of
everyone else
our lives on display we
portray a
petition for
perfection for
peace and affectation
but deep down
it's these strong
hands stealing our
breath with a
grip on our throats but
you know the secret
you know the weakness
they hide and
you know you're strong
breathe deeply and
you know you'll find
the place to hide
among the meek
among the weary
we are one
in this anti-exposure

anarchy against exploitation
we are one and
we know we will
finally find the air
to truly
breathe freely

117

this isn't a poem
I want it to be but
this is just an open mouth and a guttural choke,
gritty black vomit dripping out after hacking
coughs
hands and knees on hot asphalt dry heaving this
weakness this sea-sickness taking over after the
dizzy dance of another one-eyed night
another sunset seeping out like blood in the bath-
room sink, slippery sliding down the drain and
quickly forgotten, successfully escaped like the
circus act walking over hot coals it's been burned
away from you
calluses are the only cure to this blazing boring
black hole
this isn't a poem
I want it to be but
this is a wheel immobile, a void or a rabbit hole
with nowhere to land and if you're here with me
please hold my hand,
the end does not exist and
this is the immortal knife endlessly twisting into
my entire eternity and freedom is a fleeting feel-
ing that will only ever evade me

118

I've lost my lust for life. I used to chase sunrises and seduce sunsets with my ripe peach passion. laying in the dewy grass in the early morning and melting in flower fields in the heat of the afternoon. I followed every fantasy, fulfilled daydreams and nightmares and my tender skin felt it all.

but now my colors have faded in the hot afternoon. even sunny days look like raindrops on window panes. I wake up weak, unwelcome to the day. I move forward somehow, against a current, carrying the sorrows of yet another stranger. the future has fallen out of love with me. the moon is whispering sweetly to someone else and I hide in any shadow I can find.

I've lost my lust for life. in this weary war with myself, I've been defeated.

119

all the wild
wonderful and mild
moments
slowly begin to spin around me
a dust storm of memory
dusty dirt drying me out, filling my mouth,
choking me like the time his hands found
my throat and the time you called me worthless.
I remember feeling inferior at six years old
I remember feeling ugly at eleven when the girls on
the bus laughed at the teeth god gave me
and I hated him for it
I remember feeling for the first time
it felt like a lightning bolt
exhilarating and
changing me
forever

120

isn't it
wonderful
though?
fresh morning
after mourning
bright and new
crisp and
clear as a
summer blue.
bodies break
and bleed
but never forget
you can begin
again whenever
you need

as we wait
with hope
with each other

know this:

love remains
on the other side of the sky

so we wait
to see
with our eyes